Back in the driving seat

Overcoming fear of car travel after accidents

Sian Thrasher   Peter Hodgkinson

© CBT Networks and the authors.

The right of Sian Thrasher and Peter Hodgkinson to be identified as the authors of this work has been asserted by them in accordance with the Copyright, Designs and Patents Act of 1988.

All rights reserved. No part of this publication may be reproduced, stored in a retrieval system, or transmitted in any form or by any means without the prior written permission of the copyright owners.

Published in 2008 as an electronic book
and spiral-bound hard copy

This edition 2012 softback
ISBN 978-0-9571636-0-7

By CBT Networks
PO Box 566 Banbury
OX16 6AT
www.cbtnetworks.com

Cover photograph by John Sfondilias,
www.bigstockphoto.com

Design by Thinked
enquiries@thinked.co.uk

Contents

Chapter 1
Introduction	5
Aim of this booklet	5
Anxiety and fear	6
Golden rules for recovery	8

Chapter 2
Understanding anxiety	10
Anxiety and your body	10
The three components of anxiety	12

Chapter 3
Case histories	18

Chapter 4
What keeps your fear going?	22
Thoughts and avoidance	23
Avoidance – the vicious circle	23

Chapter 5
Relaxation	26
Control your breathing	26
Relaxing your body	27
Relaxation in the car	30

Chapter 6
Managing anxious thoughts	32
Identifying distorted thinking	32

Chapter 7
Reducing safety-seeking behaviour	44

Chapter 8
Facing the fear	56
Step 1: Set goals	58
Step 2: Build a fear hierarchy	59
Step 3. Working at your hierarchy	63

Chapter 9
Getting professional help	69
Glossary	72
Resources	74

Foreword

Fear of car travel is a common reaction to a road traffic accident, and is experienced by thousands of normal people every year. This fear may last only a week or two, but sometimes recovery takes longer. If it lasts for a month or more, then it may be helpful to actively tackle your fear in order to get your self **'back in the driving seat'** – back in control of your reactions in the car, whether as a driver or as a passenger.

The authors of this booklet have extensive experience helping people who have had accidents to overcome their fear of car travel or driving.

Dr. Sian Thrasher is a Clinical Psychologist in private practice and is Director of CBT Networks Ltd - an independent agency providing specialist psychological treatment for survivors of accidents and other traumas.

Peter Hodgkinson is a Clinical Psychologist in private practice and was Senior Partner in the Centre for Crisis Psychology.

Both authors have carried out research in the field of post-traumatic stress, and have published papers in national and international academic journals.

 Chapter 1

Introduction

Aim of this booklet

Fear of car travel or driving – sometimes referred to as a phobia[1] - is a common reaction to an accident. However, advice and help for dealing with this fear are often not readily available. This booklet aims to help you to understand fear and to give you strategies and techniques for coping with, and overcoming it

The techniques described are amongst tried and tested strategies for the management of fear. The advice given here is taken from a form of psychological (talking) treatment called Cognitive Behavioural Therapy (CBT)[1]. This booklet may be used in work with a CBT therapist. However, it may also be useful while you are awaiting therapy, or if you are coping alone.

Use what support you have available. Whether you are working on your own, or with a therapist, having a relative or close friend with whom to discuss treatment may help you to persist when it is difficult to make the changes and try the techniques recommended here.

Tackling fear is challenging. Reading this booklet may make you start to feel anxious. This is normal. Remember, you should not jump in the 'deep end' - but work through the booklet gradually, and build up your confidence one step at a time. Occasionally, working on fear of car travel may make you feel worse at first. Often this is just while

---

1   For definitions and additional reading, see Glossary

Chapter 1. Introduction

traveling, or while thinking about doing so, and should subside as you progress in your treatment. More rarely, your fear may be part of a bigger problem such as Post Traumatic Stress Disorder (PTSD)[1]. Again this is a recognized set of symptoms which form one possible emotional reaction to a traumatic event. There is good evidence that people with PTSD can benefit from the techniques described here. However, support may be needed, and you are advised to consult specialized texts on overcoming PTSD. It may be advisable to discuss additional symptoms, or persistent anxiety with a professional (see Section 10).

If in doubt, talk about it with your GP (or CBT therapist), and **never persist on your own with something that makes you feel worse for more than a day or two.**

Anxiety and fear

For many people, the main obstacle to returning to car travel after an accident is anxiety. You may use a different word to describe it: "fear", "panic", or "getting the shakes". But all these generally mean the same thing - a dread of going in the car, accompanied by unpleasant sensations in your body and by distressing thoughts.

Fear of car travel and driving following accidents is far more common than people normally realise. Feeling anxious or fearful does not make you odd in any way.

Different people experience different levels of anxiety after accidents and they feel it in different ways. Indeed, if two people from the same accident are later traveling in the same car, one may be highly anxious, while the other has no difficulty. The reason for this may not be clear, but this does not mean that the fearful person cannot take steps to regain their confidence. So, try not to feel bad if you're the one with the anxiety!

Chapter 1. Introduction

It may be that your expectations have changed. You may have enjoyed car travel or driving before the accident. If you think back, certain situations may have made you feel tense, but this only happened occasionally. After the crash, you may find that you are expecting an accident to happen **all the time**.

After an accident, some people feel reasonably relaxed when they are driving, and in control, but very nervous as a passenger, when they feel out of control. Others may refuse to get behind the wheel at all, or only drive on familiar local roads. Some may also feel anxious on other forms of transport, such as buses. None of these reactions are unusual.

Sometimes, a previous accident did not cause an anxiety reaction, and this can be very puzzling. This may be something to with the nature of the recent accident (what happened, who was in the car with you, what you thought at the time etc.) or other life pressures. But often there is no clear explanation, and worrying about 'why' may make you feel worse.

You may have simply waited for this anxiety to get better, or have already made efforts to tackle this in some way. Many people avoid driving or traveling as a passenger for a while. When they try to start traveling again, things improve a little, but then they seem to get stuck. If improvement is only very gradual, the person may not notice it, get disheartened, and give up.

The bad news about overcoming fear, is that there are no easy answers. This means that all solutions involve gradually facing your fears. The good news is that, if done in the right way, this works, and you can re-build your confidence.

This booklet provides guidelines for overcoming fear of car travel. A step-by-step approach is set out, which aims to make confidence-building as painless as possible.

Chapter 1. Introduction

The steps to progress that you will follow are:

- Understanding anxiety
- Developing coping strategies
- Graded practice.

Golden rules for recovery

Before you start work on your fears, please read and try to remember the following rules. These should help you get the most out of your program.

- EFFORT PAYS OFF

    Whether you are working with a therapist or on your own, remember that you **will only get out of treatment what you put in**. Only the 'homework practice' the therapist and you agree, or your own regular practice will make the difference. If you persist, you have a good chance of improving.

- IT WON'T ALWAYS BE PLAIN SAILING

    Don't be discouraged by setbacks. Ups and downs are normal and do not mean the program has failed. Simply go back to a lower level with which you are comfortable.

- USE ALL THE SUPPORT YOU CAN

    If you 'get stuck', talk to a friend or relative. Discuss it with your therapist who will enable you to understand the block to progress, and see if you can be helped to find a way round it.

- PAT YOURSELF ON THE BACK

    When you do something that was difficult, that counts as a success, even if you still feel somewhat fearful, so congratulate and reward yourself. You will have earned it!

Key points from Chapter 1:

- Fear of car travel after accidents is a common reaction.
- You can work on your fear alone, or with the help of a therapist.
- Follow the "Golden Rules" and you have a good chance of regaining your confidence.

Chapter 2

Understanding anxiety

Anxiety and your body

Anxiety or fear is **normal,** and in certain circumstances it is **useful.** When people are faced with difficult tasks (e.g. passing an exam, or climbing a mountain) a certain level of anxiety helps them to focus on the task in hand and to do it well.

In terms of survival, fear is a valuable reaction. When you are afraid, your body prepares itself for action – the so-called 'fight or flight' response. It has this name because it prepares you either to **fight** against a danger, or to **flee** from it. When this response is activated the following bodily changes take place:

- You breathe more quickly so that lots of oxygen can get to your brain and muscles
- Your heart beats faster so that blood is pumped round your body more quickly, again to supply your muscles with what they need
- Your muscles tense up so that you are ready to leap into action
- You sweat more because fighting or running will generate heat, and you have to get rid of that heat
- Digestion and salivation slows down because the energy for this is needed elsewhere -this may make you feel nauseous, or dry-mouthed.

Chapter 2. Understanding anxiety

Literally, the adrenaline is flowing. All these bodily changes, while uncomfortable, are **not a sign of something going wrong**. Rather, they show that your body is doing the right thing to prepare for the threat which you have perceived. These reactions have evolved to protect you, and are very useful at the right place and time. If someone were to run at you with a knife, these changes would enable you to react quickly or to run away if you needed to. In this way your body takes the necessary action for you to survive. Given the length of time the human race has been around, we can conclude that this system has been pretty successful!

Problems arise when this mechanism is set off in the wrong place, at the wrong time, or when it lasts beyond the point where it is useful.

Take the everyday example of an alarm going off at the wrong time. Car alarms are designed to protect cars from theft. Under some cases, however, the alarm will be set off when there is no thief (e.g. by the wind, or by another car passing close by). In this case the alarm is going off at the wrong time, because there is no real threat. The alarm is too sensitive. It is picking up a lot of harmless signals and reacting as though these are threatening. This is what happens during an anxiety attack, sometimes called a panic attack. Anxiety associated with car travel can be similar to this – your body's alarm signal is going off when there is no real danger.

As this alarm system has evolved over millions of years it is relatively primitive, and not under the control of the intelligent mind. Hence it is difficult consciously to switch it off. And in general, these reactions aren't harmful. If these reactions caused serious harm, the human race would have been wiped out generations ago - it would be like a car alarm that works by blowing up the car! They can feel very uncomfortable and distressing at the time, and this is of course unpleasant; but **it is only unpleasant, and not dangerous**. Furthermore, even if the alarm response does continue for a while, it cannot persist indefinitely, and in the absence of danger it fades away. You will have noticed that when you get out of the car, your fear subsides.

Chapter 2. Understanding anxiety

The challenge is to re-educate your system to understand that car travel (which, like most things in life, is not without an element of risk), is no more dangerous than before your accident, and to allow the fear response to gear down even if you stay in the driving seat.

The three components of anxiety

There are three components of anxiety. The **bodily feelings**, the cause of which you have just read about; **anxious thoughts or worries**; and **behaviours** which follow having these feelings and thoughts.

1. Bodily feelings

Common sensations associated with panic or intense anxiety are:

- Your heart beats faster, skipping beats, or palpitations
- Breathing very fast
- Feeling short of breath
- Chest pains, headaches or pains elsewhere
- Tightness in the throat
- Feeling sick or churning in the stomach
- Feeling as if you have to go to the toilet
- Feeling faint or dizzy
- Trembling or shaking
- Sweating

These are all symptoms of the 'adrenaline flowing' and we have seen that while uncomfortable, these sensations are not dangerous, but are part of our body's natural defence mechanisms. A racing heart is alarming however, leading people sometimes to think they are having a heart attack.

Strategies for managing these physical sensations are examined in Chapter 5.

Chapter 2. Understanding anxiety

2. Anxious thoughts

The way we think in a situation can strongly affect the way we feel. You may find that just considering car travel as you read this is enough to make you feel nervous – that's exactly the problem we're discussing.

Pause and think about what you are thinking….. Complete the following sentence:

| *"I don't want to go in the car because...."* | |

Negative thoughts and predictions like these are often automatic and run along without us being truly aware of how they influence us. But these thoughts have very powerful effects on how we feel and behave. They predict that something is about to go wrong, and fuel a sense of impending danger or threat. This makes us feel anxious and want to leave or avoid the situation.

Understanding the impact of your thinking on your feelings and behaviour will be important in helping you to control your fears in the car. We will look at strategies for managing anxious thoughts in Chapter 6.

3. Behaviour

Some of the thoughts you have about car travel will affect the way you behave when faced with a journey. Especially important is the tendency to **avoid** your feared situation, or to engage in behaviours which you believe help to keep you safe. **Avoidance behaviours** take us away from the feared situation. When in our feared situation we may do something to keep us safe, or to protect ourselves. This is called a '**safety-seeking behaviour**'. Avoidance and safe-seeking be-

Chapter 2. Understanding anxiety

haviours, although providing short-term relief, may have the opposite effect of keeping the fear going.

Common avoidance and safety-seeking behaviours in the car include:

Common **avoidance** behaviours:

- Avoiding car travel altogether, taking the bus or train instead
- Always letting someone else drive
- Avoiding busy roads or motorways
- Avoiding right hand turns
- Only driving in familiar places
- Avoiding driving alone
- Avoiding taxis or public transport

Common **safety-seeking** behaviours:

- Holding on to the door handle or seat, or bracing in case there is a collision
- Over-checking the mirrors or speedometer
- Gripping the steering wheel tightly
- Warning the driver to slow down
- Avoiding looking at the traffic
- Sleeping on journeys as a passenger
- Avoiding sitting in a particular seat
- Traveling only in the back seat
- Avoiding traveling with children in the car
- Taking excessively long to pull out at a junction
- Avoiding over-taking
- Pulling over towards the verge when there is oncoming traffic
- Slowing down when you see a vehicle similar to the one in the accident
- Avoiding driving at night or in the rain

Notice that some of these safety-seeking behaviours might in fact be hazardous!

In the short-term, these attempts to reduce your fear seem to make you feel better. It is natural to want to avoid something you think is threatening. In fact, avoidance would be the correct thing to do if you were actually in danger. However, after an accident, many people over-estimate the actual risk associated with car travel. Importantly, by avoiding car travel, you are making it **hard to find out whether or not it is as dangerous as you think.** You never learn that it is okay, and that you do survive.

Similarly, if when you are in the car, you do a lot of things to make you 'feel safer' - repeatedly checking the mirrors, watching the speedometer, gripping on, shouting out warnings to the driver - you can **never find out whether you would have arrived or completed the journey safely without doing these things**. You are convincing yourself that checking or back seat driving helped you to arrive safely. This maintains your fears.

No matter how much you practice being in the car, safety-seeking behaviours will stop you getting used to it because your system thinks it is still dangerous, otherwise why would you still be gripping on, or for instance avoiding driving in town?

It is important to note that, some avoidance or safety-seeking behaviours may in fact be making you *less* safe in the car. For example, as a passenger, shouting at the driver can be distracting, and on the 'crying wolf' principle means that on that very rare occasion when you do need to warn the driver of something, they may not pay any attention. As a driver, over-checking the rear view mirror means you are not looking at the road ahead.

In summary safety-seeking behaviour maintains your fear, and may itself be dangerous. Reducing safety-seeking behaviour (and still driving safely) will be explored in Chapter 7.

Chapter 2. Understanding anxiety

Beware of your inner critic!

If you notice that your thoughts or behaviour have changed since the accident, you may be tempted to tell yourself off, or call yourself "stupid" or "weak". This critical part of ourselves might be called our "inner critic". Sometimes our inner critic can be useful. For example, this warning inner voice may spur us on to get up in time to get to work in the morning, despite a desire to stay in bed longer. When it comes to working on your fears, your inner critic may motivate you start to make a change.

However, your inner critic may also make you think: "I'm stupid, no one else reacts like this." Beating yourself up about having become fearful is not helpful. **Try not to judge or condemn yourself for being fearful.** As we have said, fear of car travel is a common experience for thousands of normal people every year. Blaming yourself for it will probably only make you feel worse.

Instead, try to develop an **encouraging inner voice**. You could try saying to yourself, *"I'm working on it"*, or *"One step at a time"*. It is hard work facing your fears, and it takes courage and determination to start thinking about change. Congratulate yourself for facing up to the challenge of re-building your confidence.

Key Points from Chapter 2:

- Fear is normal.
- There are physical symptoms of anxiety which are uncomfortable but not harmful.
- It is difficult to switch off an anxiety alarm which has become sensitive to certain situations e.g. car travel.
- There are 3 components of anxiety - bodily feelings, anxious thoughts, and behaviour.

Chapter 2. Understanding anxiety

- Avoidance behaviours and safety-seeking behaviour may make us feel better in the short-term, but in the long-run may keep our anxiety going, or make it worse.
- All 3 components of anxiety need to be managed in order to overcome fear.
- Re-building confidence is a challenge, and you should congratulate yourself for facing up to it and making a start.

 Chapter 3

Case histories

Here are some case histories of people involved in car accidents. You may see some similarities with your difficulties in these people's problems.

Carol

Carol was a rear seat passenger in the family car. Her husband was driving. She saw headlights coming towards them and there was a head on collision. No one was injured.

Two months later the family got a new car. During this time Carol did not travel in a car at all, although she could have. Instead, she preferred to take the train. When the new car came, it was several weeks before she would get in it as a passenger, and she only began to drive again some 6 months later. She was aware that she was avoiding driving out of fear.

Even when she did start driving again, Carol would only take essential journeys as a passenger or a driver, and would refuse to go out at night (the accident had happened at night). Unfortunately, they then had another small "bump" which was not frightening, and Carol continued driving afterwards. However, a few days later, the car was off the road for 2 or 3 weeks, receiving some mechanical attention, and Carol did not drive it after this. Following the second "bump", and the gap in driving, she had begun to think that accidents were more likely to happen again.

Carol was at her worst as a passenger. She described the journey to a family gathering as "terrifying" saying: "It was along country lanes, and every time I saw headlights I felt so scared that I just wanted to get out". She said: "I am very aware of other cars", watching oncoming traffic to see if it is "too far over towards the middle of the road". If a car is too near the middle, she notes: "My heart jumps violently, I get sweaty palms. I hang on to the seat belt and shout at the driver to watch out!"
Over 4 months some symptoms gradually improved with the help of breathing techniques to aid relaxation. Carol practiced her breathing techniques using a tape and written instructions (see Chapter 5). She learned to relax more as a passenger and cut down on unnecessary warnings. With practice, fear reduced and confidence grew. Carol said "It's a lot easier now in the dark than it was... It's not so bad on big roads, where there is plenty of room for passing cars".

Jane

Jane was waiting to turn right on her way to work, when she saw a bus close to her left. She thought "He must have seen me", but the bus hit her car on the left side. Afterwards, her heart was racing, she could not get her breath, and she was shaking. However, she drove on to work.

Jane never avoided driving. For a number of months she was very wary when drawing up alongside cars or buses. She was nervous about whether people had seen her or not, and felt that her left side was very vulnerable. She would always be checking what was to her left, and described herself as "obsessional". She feared being "sandwiched", having vehicles to both left and right, and avoided driving in the middle lane, or in queued traffic. About her fear she predicted "I couldn't stand it". When these sorts of things happened, she would feel sick and shaky. When coming up to a junction, where she expected to feel "sandwiched", she would change lanes to avoid this. She also found herself very wary of buses, lorries or any other big vehicles, and would be nervous at roundabouts where she was "extremely cautious", repeatedly checking her mirrors and waiting until all other vehicles had gone. This hyper-vigilance and safety-seeking behaviour lasted for a few months, but her driving then gradually returned to normal.

Philip

Philip was driving along a dual carriageway, with his 4 year old son in the back of the car. Another vehicle turned through the central reservation in front of him and he could not avoid hitting it.

Following the accident, Philip had no particular anxiety in the car on local trips. Long distance driving was a problem for him, especially on dual carriageways or motorways where the speed of other vehicles worried him. He found such journeys "horrendous" especially when his son was in the car. If he could find a way to avoid motorways, he would. On busy roads he would develop pain in his jaw as a result of muscular tension, and this got worse the longer he spent in the car. As a driver, he was more cautious, driving more slowly, and being very vigilant.

As a passenger he was "ninety times worse". His wife described how, when he was anxious, he would put his hands on the dashboard, watch the speedometer, and if anything untoward happened, he would shout. Philip found that when he was a passenger, he would break into a sweat, and his heart would race. His behaviour in the car caused arguments with his wife. To cap it all, his son had become nervous about car travel, too, probably through seeing both his father frightened, and experiencing the shouting between his parents on journeys.

Chapter 3. Case histories

Tony

Tony had never been a driver, and had never attempted to learn. One day, being driven by his wife, a car came out of a side turning, and hit the passenger door. Tony was very panicky and distressed at the scene and was badly bruised.

It was a week before he was physically able to go out again. On his first trip in the car to the supermarket, he had a severe panic attack; crying and sweating, his heart pounding - he was terrified. He tried it once more the next week, with the same result. He vowed he would never go in the car again. It can be easily imagined how this altered family life. He had to take the bus to work, and to the shops, and could not go out with the family at the weekend. They had to cancel a holiday in Scotland.

After a year, there had been no change in his problem. Hearing of accidents on the news only reinforced his belief that cars are dangerous, and should be avoided at all costs.

Chapter 4

What keeps your fear going?

We have discussed the three components of anxiety – bodily feelings, anxious thoughts and behaviours. And we have referred to the way behaviours and thoughts maintain fear. Let's summarise the three main reasons why fear persists:

- **Negative predictions** or thoughts about car travel may lead to an exaggerated perception of danger. You may not even be aware of this.

- When you **avoid**, or largely avoid the situations you fear, the fear either stays the same, or gets worse.

- If you use excessive **safety-seeking behaviours** in the car, you never learn that you would be safe without them.

Anxious thoughts and avoidance behaviours prepare you to be easily **resensitised**. By this we mean that when a situation occurs, such as a vehicle ahead braking unexpectedly, which before the accident you would have easily dismissed, it now feeds your anxiety further. Your perceptions of danger are reinforced, your safety-seeking behaviours are maintained, and the adrenaline flow continues at inappropriate times.

Chapter 4. What keeps your fear going?

Thoughts and avoidance

As we have said, if you become fearful of driving after an accident, you may try to avoid car travel as much as possible, or restrict yourself to short journeys on familiar local routes, because you think that this will reduce the likelihood of another accident happening that way.

You may think *"Cars are dangerous, and I can't bear being in them anymore"*. The first part of this statement can't be contradicted, of course. Cars (like many things in this world) are dangerous in certain circumstances. However, every day we do many things which are dangerous **without thinking about the danger**. The problem is that our fearful thinking has become **exaggerated**. Because we have had one accident, we over-anticipate the possibility of another. Avoiding car travel means that exaggerated thinking is never proven incorrect.

It is natural to avoid something which makes you feel uncomfortable, and in the short-term you might feel relieved and more relaxed by avoiding car travel. In the long-term, however, avoiding does not get rid of the problem, and for some people things can get worse and worse, with them becoming frightened of more and more situations.

It is normal to want to protect yourself when you feel at risk, but putting up the protective screen prevents you finding out what would happen without it.

Avoidance – the vicious circle

The principle of avoidance is this: **If each time you avoid a feared situation, you feel better, then it is more likely that the next time the feared situation crops up, you will avoid it again.** At the same time you never learn that you can cope with the feared situation, and the fear remains. Literally, this is a vicious circle.

Chapter 4. What keeps your fear going?

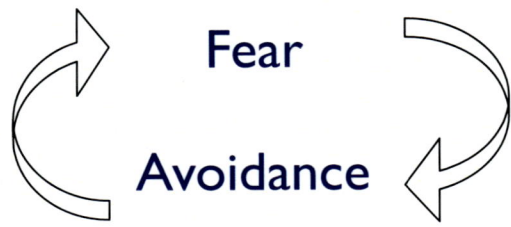

Now, answer this question:

What would happen if you did something you find hard, like face a situation you find frightening for a longer time, rather than cut your time as short as possible? Would your anxiety …	a) Get worse b) Stay the same c) Decrease

Based on your experience to date, you would probably say "Get worse", or "Stay the same". You may think it would get so bad that you would be overwhelmed, or pass out.

But these answers are not necessarily correct. In most feared situations, after a certain time, anxiety begins to **decrease of its own accord. If you leave the situation as quickly as you can, you never find this out.**

The principle behind all treatment of anxiety like this is:

If you are prepared to tolerate your anxiety in the car, and you learn how to manage your anxious thoughts and feelings, your anxiety will decrease over time.

To achieve this you will have to:

- Learn skills of coping with anxious thoughts and feelings
- Identify and gradually reduce safety-seeking behaviour
- Be prepared to enter the feared situations in a step-by-step fashion (least anxiety provoking first)
- Repeat this until your fear begins to drop.

Do not worry that becoming very frightened will be harmful. Fear, though uncomfortable, will not hurt you. Remember, it is a simple physical response to perceived danger and your 'anxiety alarm' is going off at the wrong time.

The next two chapters outline coping strategies for managing anxiety and managing anxious thoughts. These techniques are aimed at making it possible to begin facing your fears. **It is facing your fear which will make the most impact on your confidence in the car.**

Key Points from Chapter 4:

- Fear is kept going by negative predictions and thoughts, avoidance and safety-seeking behaviour.
- It is normal to want to avoid or protect yourself when you feel at risk, but if you leave a situation as quickly as you can, you never find out that in most cases your anxiety will decrease of its own accord after a certain time.
- The `protective` screen of safety behaviour prevents you from finding out what would happen without it.
- If you are prepared to tolerate your anxiety and you learn how to manage your thoughts and feelings, your fear will decrease over time.
- Facing your fear will make the most impact on your confidence in the car.

Chapter 5. Relaxation

 Chapter 5

Relaxation

In learning to manage anxiety, it is important to learn which are good coping strategies, and which are not helpful. Unhelpful coping would include relying on alcohol or tranquillizers, avoiding difficult situations, telling your self off, being a back seat driver, etc.

There are a number of helpful coping strategies for controlling fear. You may like to try these and use one or more to help you through the program. Relaxation is particularly useful, but different techniques suit different people. They all require practice. Studies suggest that working on avoidance behaviour is often the most effective means of overcoming fear, but these anxiety management techniques can be a useful tool to help you manage the uncomfortable feelings caused by anxiety.

Step 1   Take some time to read through the following exercises;
Step 2   Try out each technique;
Step 3   Practice regularly the techniques which you find most beneficial/comfortable.

Control your breathing

As we discussed earlier, when you are feeling panicky, you will start to breathe more quickly so that your heart can pump more oxygen around your body. This means your muscles will be ready for action. Unfortunately, breathing too fast and deeply can lead to more anxiety symptoms, such as faintness, chest pain, tingling and dizziness. If

Chapter 5. Relaxation

breathing can be controlled during anxiety, unpleasant symptoms may be reduced. If you breathe calmly and slowly, the alarm bell should stop ringing.

To help yourself, practice the following breathing exercises *daily*, starting at home, when you feel calm and relaxed.

> 1) Fill your lungs with air. Your stomach should push out too. This should feel quite tight as your muscles stretch. Do rot breathe in a shallow way from your upper chest, try to breathe filling your lower half with air first (and sticking out your tummy).
>
> 2) As you slowly breathe in, count "1 and 2 and 3 and 4" in your head. Then let that breath out, counting slowly to six "1 and 2 and 3 and 4 and 5 and 6". Do this 3 or 4 times, until your breathing calms down, and then breathe normally, concentrating on the feelings of relaxation.

Breathing exercises can be practiced sitting stationary in the car.

Relaxing your body

Learning to physically relax when you are *not* in the car, can help you to relax when you *are* in the car. The instructions for relaxation are given below.

- To start with, you will need to set aside 15 minutes per day to practice relaxation
- Try to pick the same time every day - a time when you won't be disturbed
- Sit in a comfortable chair, with your head and arms supported
- Loosen ties, belts, etc - take off your shoes and get comfortable
- Close your eyes
- Try not to fidget

Chapter 5. Relaxation

Use a relaxation tape to guide you through the exercises. Your therapist may have given you one, or you can order your own - see Resources section for details.

The basic exercises:

Even without a tape you can work your way through the following exercises to get an idea of how it feels to relax different parts of your body. With practice you can learn to physically relax your body at time so stress and anxiety. This will be a useful tool when overcoming your fears.

1. LOWER ARMS
Make a tight fist with each hand and feel the tension round the knuckles and up the forearm (don't let your fingernails dig in to you palms).
Hold for 2 - 3 seconds and then release. As you relax, let your arms sink down on the arm of the chair.
Now relax, and concentrate on the feelings of relaxation in the muscles. Say to yourself "Relax".

2. UPPER ARMS
Push your elbows into the arm of the chair. Do not tense the lower arms, leave them loose, but feel the tension in your upper arms. Now "Relax".

3. FACE
Do these 3 exercises together:
(i) Raise your eyebrows as far as possible with your eyes closed. (Not too hard or your eyes will ache). Feel the tension in your forehead.
(ii) Screw up your eyes and wrinkle your nose. Feel the tension in your cheeks and around your eyes.
(iii) Push back the corners of your mouth in a grimace (don't worry, nobody is looking!). Feel the tension in you cheeks and jaws. Now "Relax".

4. Neck
Push your chin down towards your chest, but try and prevent it from actually touching. Feel the tension in your neck.
Now "Relax".

5. Chest, Shoulders and Back
Push your shoulders back into the chair and feel the tension in your chest, shoulders and upper back.
Now "Relax".

6. Stomach
Pull in your tummy muscles, and hold your breath, releasing it as you relax.
Now "Relax".

7. Legs
Right leg first - straighten your whole leg by lifting it off the ground and point your big toe in towards your body to make a right angle as you stretch your foot. Feel the tension all down your leg, then let it sink down to the floor.
Repeat this with the other leg.
Now "Relax".

The more you practice these exercises, the more automatic the relaxation will become. Eventually you should be able to loosen all your muscles at once, just by telling yourself to 'Relax'. You can try relaxing in all sorts of situations e.g. the bus stop, the supermarket queue. No one will notice!

Chapter 5. Relaxation

Relaxation in the car

Relaxation in the car - stationary

Now, you need to try relaxing in the car. Try the following exercise while sitting in a stationary car with the engine off:

1. Sit with your hands on your lap, or the wheel, and your feet on the pedals or floor
2. Give your level of anxiety or tension a rating between 0 an 10 (where 0 is "completely relaxed" and 10 is "totally panicked")
3. Notice where in your body you feel tense
4. Release the tension, by clenching and relaxing that particular muscle group with the exercise you have practiced
5. As a passenger practice putting your hands loosely in your lap, and relaxing your feet and legs. As a driver, put your hands on the wheel and practice tensing and relaxing your arm and hand muscles, and tensing and relaxing your feet over the pedals. Try and recall how you used to feel traveling by car, before you became fearful
6. Tell yourself to "Relax"
7. Stay in the situation, repeating stages 1-6 until your anxiety rating reduces to 3 or below

Repeat the exercise with the car engine running, sitting in a different seat, or with the car parked where you can watch traffic come and go.

Relaxation in the car - moving

When you can relax in a stationary car, you can try to relax while the car is moving.

Firstly, both as a passenger and driver, you need to become more aware of tension building. So, how do you know when you are excessively tense? What are the warning signs e.g. headache, pain in shoulders? Compare how you feel in your body in the car now, with how you felt before the accident. Ask yourself to what degree current physical tension is useful? Now, work on cutting down the excess tension with the following exercises.

As a passenger, practice letting your hands and legs go floppy. Even when you feel fearful, behave as though you are relaxed. This gives your system a clear message that clinging on, or bracing for impact is not necessary. In the long run this should help to gear down your fear alarm.

As a driver, start with a relatively easy or familiar journey, and without compromising safety, become aware of any physical tension in your body while driving along. Check for tension in your shoulders, hands, arms and legs, and gently try to release it. Rate your level of tension on a 0-10 scale. Then try to release some of the tension. Let your shoulders drop, and reduce excessive pressure in your grip on the wheel.

Of course, a certain amount of tension and alertness when driving is desirable. The aim here is to reduce excessive tension, or tension which is not helpful.

Key Points from Chapter 5:

- Relaxation training can be a useful technique for coping with anxiety.
- You can learn to control your breathing by practicing regular exercises.
- Learn Progressive Muscular Relaxation using a tape or by following the written exercises given above.
- Once you learn to relax at home, you can start to become aware of physical tension when you are in the car, and work on releasing it by tensing and relaxing different muscle groups (being careful not to compromise safety).

 Chapter 6

Managing anxious thoughts

The first step to modifying your anxious thinking is to become aware of it. This is not as easy as it sounds, and needs practice. The second step is to try to work out whether your anxious thoughts are realistic. If they are exaggerated or distorted, then you need to look for more realistic ways of thinking.

Identifying distorted thinking

In any situation there is more than one way of interpreting what is happening. When you are anxious you are more likely to jump to the most frightening interpretation. If you can identify distorted thinking, then you have the opportunity to reduce fear-provoking thoughts, to develop a more balanced viewpoint, and this will help you to feel more confident.

Exercise One

Over the next week, keep a record of what goes through your mind when you go in the car or think about going in the car. There may be certain words or statements, or images that come when you are nervous. Write down whatever is in your mind when you are anxious, and keep a 'Thought Record' in order to identify any patterns or repeated themes in your thinking (see below).

Daily Thought Record

SITUATION:	**Invited to a friend's for lunch**	
EMOTIONS	AUTOMATIC THOUGHTS	CHALLENGE TO THOUGHTS
Specify: •What are you feeling? •Rate the strength of your feelings (0-10)	•Write down the thoughts that went through your mind just before you experienced the feelings •For each thought, rate how much you believed it at that moment	•How certain are you that this thought is correct? (0-100%) •Is it a helpful thought for you to have at this point in time?
Fear (8)	*"If I drive to my friend's house, I may be in another accident" (7)*	*I am not certain that this is true, but I feel in danger (50%) It is not helpful.*

Chapter 6. Managing anxious thoughts

	"I won't enjoy the lunch as I'll be worried about the return journey the whole time" (10)	I am certain this is true, although I may be able to forget about the journey and enjoy seeing my friend for some of the time (65%). The thought makes me feel like staying at home, which is not helpful, as I am losing touch with my friends.

There are several common thinking errors associated with fear, and your thinking will probably fall into the following general categories. Note 'yes' or 'no' in the box against each category which seems familiar, or which comes up in your thought record, and write down an example in the space provided.

Anticipatory thoughts	
Yes/No	These are worries about what might happen in some future situation, e.g. "If I ask for a lift, and we have an accident, it will be all my fault" *Yes*
My example	*If I drive somewhere & I can't do it. I'll be a failure*

Chapter 6. Managing anxious thoughts

Awfulisation	
Yes/No	These thoughts involve dire predictions that something awful is going to happen, e.g. *"…It will be terrible. We'll all be killed on the motorway. We won't make it there alive. I can't cope with the worry"* no/sometimes
My example	If I'd been driving…. (would be much worse)
Hyper-vigilant thoughts	
Yes/No	These are thoughts which come from keeping on the lookout for danger when traveling in the car. Most of them are about your constant looking to see what is happening on the road, e.g. *"Oh, God, look at that car at that junction… He's not seen us… He's going too fast. He'll never stop in time. It's my side of the car he'll hit… We're going to crash!* Yes
My example	When a passenger in the car with mum, I'm constantly monitoring other drives + am very hyper vigilant

Chapter 6. Managing anxious thoughts

'Fear of fear' thoughts	
Yes/No	These are thoughts about the consequences of physical symptoms of anxiety. Once you get physically het-up, the following thoughts may arise: *"Oh no, I'm sweating again…My heart's going…I just can't bear this… It's horrible…. I'll have a heart attack if it goes on like this… I'm getting dizzy… I'll pass out".* *no*
My example	

Escape thoughts	
Yes/No	These thoughts lead to avoidance: *"Which way can I turn? I must get onto a quieter road"* or *"I've got to get out… This journey must be over soon… Shall I ask her to stop the car so I can get out? I'll be OK if I can just get out and calm down".* *Yes*
My example	*You drive (to Mum) then a sense of relief*

Chapter 6. Managing anxious thoughts

Self-critical thoughts	
Yes/No	These are the condemnatory thoughts with which people think about their fears and their coping, or, as they see it, lack of it, e.g. *"You fool... it was only a silly accident... you should be dealing with it better than this... You shouldn't be getting so upset, you should be able to drive to the party. You used to be so strong... and now you're weak and pathetic!"*
My example	Yes — Putting self down & laughing at self

Modifying Distorted Thinking

It may be possible to identify some patterns in your thinking associated with car travel. Even if your thoughts are different from the examples given, it is possible to look for other ways of seeing things. Try the following exercises in order to work on more realistic or more helpful alternatives to the fear-provoking interpretations. You are aiming to put your negative thinking "on trial" in order to try to develop a more balanced and confident viewpoint.

Exercise One

The following questions may help you generate less alarming, and more balanced ways of thinking about being in the car.

Chapter 6. Managing anxious thoughts

- **ARE MY FEARS BASED ON FACT OR JUST OPINION?**

    Try to stand back, and ask your self whether the thoughts you have identified are facts, with which most other people would agree, or whether they are opinions, distorted by your fear. Ask yourself what you would think if you were more confident in the car, like you used to be? How would someone else see the situation?

- **IS THERE ANY EVIDENCE AGAINST MY THINKING?**

    You might ask a friend or partner to help you come up with evidence that contradicts your worry.

- **IS THERE AN ALTERNATIVE OR MORE HELPFUL WAY OF SEEING THINGS?**

- **HOW LIKELY IS ANOTHER ACCIDENT?**

    If you fear being in another accident, then work out the probability i.e. since learning to drive how many journeys have you completed per week, per month, per year? What is that total? How many accidents have you had in this time? Express the total number of accidents as a percentage of the total number of journeys. (Hint: use a calculator to work out the rough figures).

- **WHAT WERE THE ACTUAL CAUSES OF THE ACCIDENT YOU WERE IN?**

    Do you have a sense that you are jinxed? Is there a chance that your sense of responsibility or blame for the accident is exaggerated? To check this out, try writing down a list of the factors which added together resulted in there being an accident, e.g. bad weather, the other driver taking the bend too fast, the other driver's lack of concentration, the lack of street lights, etc. When you have set them all out, put them in order – most important factor in contributing to the accident at the top, least important at the bottom – marking which you think are down to you, and

Chapter 6. Managing anxious thoughts

which you had no control over. You could calculate the percentage that you think each contributes to the cause of the accident, and then calculate what percentage is directly attributable to you.

> **Case example:**
>
> Kevin had been involved in a road traffic accident on the motorway, as a result of which he suffered serious injuries to his legs. Over time his physical injuries healed, but he remained anxious driving, and avoided motorways altogether. He identified the following negative thoughts:
>
> *"If I drive down the motorway, I will be in another accident".*
> *"If I am in another accident I will be paralysed or killed and my children will not have a father".*
> *"I have been lucky once, but I won't be lucky next time"*
> *"If I had been careful, I wouldn't be in this position (chronic pain, unable to play football)"*
>
> Kevin used the following technique to check out the thought "If I had been more careful, I would not be in this position"
>
> STEP 1.
> Kevin made a list of all the factors which lead to the crash. To do this he thought through the sequence of events in the crash carefully, and made the following list:
>
> *FACTORS WHICH LED TO THE CRASH*
> 1. Busy motorway
> 2. Lorry driver pulling out without indicating
> 3. No way I could escape because traffic in outside lane

Chapter 6. Managing anxious thoughts

For each factor, he estimated the degree to which it caused the crash in terms of a percentage:

1. Busy motorway	10%
2. Lorry driver pulling out without indicating	80%
3. No way I could escape because traffic in outside lane	10%

Kevin used a "Responsibility cake" or pie chart to visualize this:

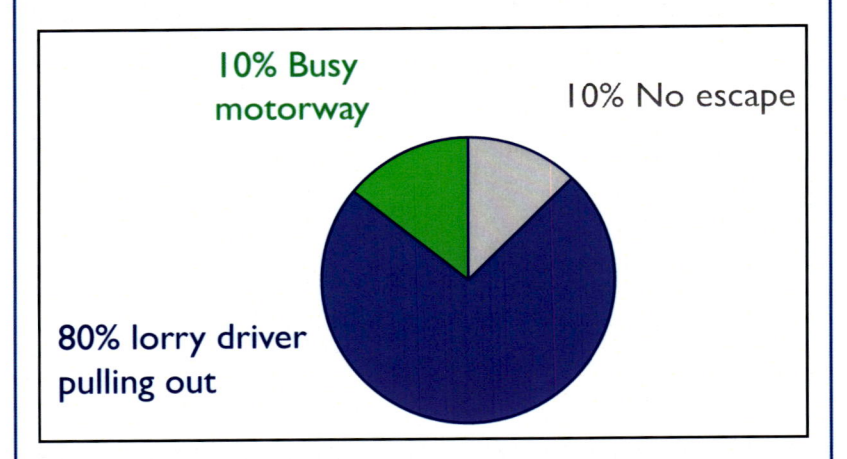

10% Busy motorway

10% No escape

80% lorry driver pulling out

CONCLUSION:

Kevin concluded that the lorry driver pulling out without indicating was the major cause of the crash.

Chapter 6. Managing anxious thoughts

Exercise Two

Use the following steps to generate a challenge to your negative thought or an alternative way of seeing things. It is important that your challenge is a more positive, balanced and realistic alternative. Ask yourself the following questions in order to find a challenge to each thought:

1) What is an alternative way of looking at this?
2) How would someone else see the situation? (Ask a friend.)
3) Is there any real evidence that this is likely to happen?
4) Is this a real fear, or is it unfounded because there is no evidence to support it?
5) What are the chances of this happening?
6) Am I basing my worry on an isolated incident?
7) Am I generalizing from one bad experience to all car journeys? How many have actually been safe?

In your thought record, write down a rational alternative way of seeing things – a challenge to your negative thoughts - based on real evidence.

Practice reading this over, and saying it to yourself, firstly when you are calm, and then in the car.

Case example:

Theresa is fearful driving because she thinks "If I get lost, I'll panic and be unable to find my way home"

She explores the evidence for and against this prediction using the table below:

Chapter 6. Managing anxious thoughts

Evidence for prediction	Evidence against prediction
1) I get nervous in the car	1) I have never been unable to get home before even when really upset
2) When I panic I find it difficult to think straight	1) If I am panicky I can pull over and calm down 2) I can use a map or take my mobile phone if I get really lost

Thought challenging is not as simple as it looks. **It is a skill which needs practice**. You may intellectually know that your thinking is distorted, but be unable to shift the feeling that your bias is true. This is normal. It will take time for your fear response to gear down. Fearful thinking has a tendency to persist even when you know better. It is as though your system has developed a bias towards more negative predictions "just in case" something dangerous happens. Your fear is part of a system designed to protect you, but which is misguided. It is working on a "better safe than sorry" principle and over-estimating the chances of harm occurring to yourself. And of course if the threat were as severe or as common as your fear system is predicting, then that would be useful. For example, it is useful to be wary of precipitous cliff edges. In the case of car travel, while it is not 100% risk free, it is probably not as dangerous as your fears are telling you (check this out using the questions in the box above).

The techniques described above are taken from a Cognitive Behavioural approach to treating anxiety. Traditionally this kind of work is undertaken with the help of a specially trained Cognitive Behavioural Therapist. It is to be hoped that you can begin to use these techniques independently. However, if you get stuck, you may benefit from the support from a CBT therapist in order to help you identify negative thoughts and biases, and develop alternative, and more realistic challenges (see Glossary and Resources sections for more information on finding a therapist).

Key Points from Chapter 6:

- The first step to modifying anxious thinking is to become aware of it
- A "Thought Record" can be helpful to identify patterns of fears in your thinking
- Finding more realistic or helpful alternatives to fear-provoking thoughts can be achieved using questions which challenge these thoughts
- Thought challenging takes practice and you may benefit from the support of a CBT Therapist

Chapter 7

Reducing safety-seeking behaviour

As explained in Chapter 2, safety-seeking behaviours (like over-checking the mirrors, warning the driver, etc.) may make you feel safer in the short-term, but in the long-term may be maintaining your fears. You never learn that driving has *not* become more dangerous since the accident. Being over-cautious can itself put you in danger. In overcoming your fears, it is important to wean yourself off safety-seeking behaviours.

Become aware of your behaviours

As with anxious thinking, the first step is to become aware of any changes in your behaviour in the car since the accident.

- Write a list of all the safety-seeking behaviours you are aware of or tick the boxes against the common safety-seeking behaviours listed below. Use the spaces if there are things you do which are not listed (there are too many to mention here).

- Ask a partner or friend which of behaviours from the list they have noticed

- Keep a diary of safety-seeking behaviours over a week.

Chapter 7. Reducing safety-seeking behaviour

Common safety-seeking behaviours	
Tick	**As a passenger**
	Gripping on to the handle or seat
	Shouting out warnings to the driver e.g. to slow down
	Pressing an imaginary brake
	Checking the rear (e.g. using wing or visor mirrors)
	Scanning the road ahead for potential hazards
	Bracing for impact
	Only sitting in a the back or front seat
	Leaning right back in seat at junctions
	Checking the speedometer
Tick	**As driver**
	Over-checking rearview mirror
	Scanning the road ahead intensely
	Gripping on to the wheel tightly at potential hazards
	Spending hours planning a route, or checking a map before leaving the house
	Avoid driving outside "safe" zone
	Taking excessive time to pull out at a junction or roundabout
	Only traveling when accompanied
	Insisting on complete silence in the car

Chapter 7. Reducing safety-seeking behaviour

Tick	**General:**
	Always carrying a mobile phone, even on short journeys (just in case)
	Asking loved ones to "check in" by phone when they reach their destination by car
	Repeatedly warning other drivers to be careful before they go out in the car, or getting them to phone home when they have arrived safely.
	Repeated checking of child seats (more than once)

Challenging safety-seeking behaviours

You should now be familiar with the idea of challenging thoughts.

A lot of people think safety-seeking behaviours are simply sensible. So how can we tell when what we are doing is excessive, or fear-maintaining? If you are not sure whether what you are doing in the car is a safety-seeking behaviour, ask yourself the following questions:

- WHAT IS THE AIM OF MY BEHAVIOUR? DOES THIS BEHAVIOUR MAKE THE JOURNEY SAFER?

    If the aim is purely to make you feel less anxious and is only a response to fear, and it is clear that it is not actually making you safer, then it is a safety-seeking behaviour. You could check this out with a friend if you are not sure.

    For example, if I grip on to the seat whenever the driver goes around a corner, this is a response to fear. It does not actually make me any safer, and will reinforce my fears that I am in imminent danger. Similarly, only sitting in the rear seats (rather than the front) does not actually make the journey safer. But it does stop me finding out that I can travel safely as a front seat passenger too.

- MIGHT THIS BEHAVIOUR MAKE THE JOURNEY LESS SAFE?

  In some cases there are clear disadvantages to the behaviour. Thus, grabbing the driver's arm can in itself be dangerous. Shouting warnings can distract the driver rather than alerting them to danger. Excessive rear-view mirror checking can interfere with concentrating on the road ahead.

- HOW DID I BEHAVE BEFORE THE ACCIDENT?

  Is there a change from how you used to behave before the accident? Was that old way of behaving a mistake? Does the change mean you are safer now, or just more nervous?

- WHAT DOES YOUR PARTNER OR FRIEND THINK?

  Talk to someone whom you know to be a sensible driver, and ask for their opinion. You could consult a driving school for information on best practice, or even consider a defensive driving course.

Some things to consider

In some situations the decision as to what is really safe and sensible, and what is excessive may be less clear-cut. As a passenger, it may be unhelpful to shout out at the driver at every imagined or potential hazard. However, at times it may be useful to be a second pair of eyes (e.g. if the driver appears not to have seen the lights change to red). At these times, warning the driver is the sensible thing to do.

What is sensible driving behaviour may vary depending on the type of journey you are making (motorway or town), or what the road conditions are like (busy or quiet, foggy or clear). Take the example of mirror-checking. When you are driving down winding country lanes, excessive checking of the rear-view mirror may be unnecessary, and possibly even dangerous, as your attention is away from the road ahead. However, on the motorway it is good practice to check your mirrors regularly and always before manoeuvering. There may be no exact right and wrong here, but instead it will be a case of judgment. Where you are uncertain, check it out with friends or family, or you may wish to consult with a qualified driving instructor.

Reducing excessive safety-seeking behaviours

If you have noticed some excessive safety-seeking behaviours, the next step is to start to reduce them.

There are several **general rules for reducing excessive safety-seeking behaviour**:

- Decide which safety-seeking behaviours are definitely excessive, and choose one at a time to work on, starting with the easiest.

- Reducing safety-seeking behaviour may initially make you feel slightly more nervous. Grading the behaviours in terms of how difficult or anxiety-provoking it will be to try to reduce them will make this easier.

- Start by tackling the easiest first, moving on to the next one in a step-by-step fashion.

- Decide what your goal is e.g. to shout out at the driver less, to grip on less.

- If you wish to reduce the frequency of a behaviour, choose a journey you make regularly e.g. to work or to the supermarket, and the next time you make that journey, count how many times

Chapter 7. Reducing safety-seeking behaviour

you grip on. Try to reduce this number each time you complete that journey.

- It is a good idea to tell your partner or friend what you are doing, so that they can support or remind you, and congratulate you when you are managing to relax more in the car.

Case Example:

In order to work on his excessive mirror checking, Tom used the following challenges to his negative automatic thoughts:

Negative Thought	Challenge
"If I don't look in the mirror, then I will be hit from behind"	Is there an alternative way of looking at this? Does checking a lot really reduce the risk? Is there a problem with excessive checking?

Tom came up with the following alternatives:

Even if I had checked the mirror in my accident, I could not have prevented the vehicle hitting me from behind.

Checking the mirror at traffic lights does not prevent a shunt as I could not take evasive action anyway.

By looking in the mirror excessively, I am not concentrating on the road ahead, and may be putting other drivers at risk.

Chapter 7. Reducing safety-seeking behaviour

The strategies available for cutting down excessive safety-seeking behaviour depend on whether you are a passenger or a driver.

Reducing excessive safety-seeking behaviour as a passenger

When reducing excessive safety-behaviour as a passenger, try the following techniques:

a) relaxation
b) response prevention
c) deliberate distraction

a) Relaxation

You should by now be familiar with relaxation techniques. If you tend to grip on to the door handle, or clench you hands etc. you might decide to hold your hands loosely in you lap instead. This is easier said than done and needs practice. The aim is for you to try to behave as if you are relaxed, even if at first you do not feel so. Try to be aware of tension in your body by checking yourself according to the muscle groups you relax in the exercises (see Chapter 5): hands, arms, face, neck, shoulders, tummy, legs. If you feel tense in your shoulders at traffic lights, try taking a deep breath and relax that muscle group. This acts as a distraction in its own right.

b) Response prevention

Example 1

As a passenger, you may by now have become accustomed to checking to the rear, for example. You may do this by turning. Some passengers adjust the door mirror so they can see to the rear, or have the visor down so they can use that mirror. If so, you might usefully make the decision to cut this behaviour out. Readjust the mirror for the driver's use and put the visor up so that they are not available to you. This is what is called **response prevention** i.e. actively preventing yourself from carrying out a behaviour and not responding to your urge to escape the situation, or to avoid feeling fear by engaging in a behaviour which is of no real use. After all, it is the driver's job to check the rear. Only by stopping this excessive checking, do you find out that you are just as safe without it. You may feel more fearful when you first cut down on excessive checking, but with practice, the urge to do it will pass.

Example 2

Fearful passengers typically warn the driver more and may shout out. Thus, in order to gear down your anxiety, you will need to stop yourself from doing this. You will need to "zip it" or bite your lip!

Remember, the general rule is that if you want to feel relaxed and confident as a passenger, then you have to *behave as though you are relaxed and confident*. Some people refer to this as "walking the talk". You know it makes sense to change your behaviour, but you may feel uncomfortable until you get used to doing things differently. It is possible to behave as though you are confident, even when you are nervous. For example, when you first arrive at a party you may feel shy and awkward. However, if you behave confidently, start a conversation with someone, or join in the dancing, you begin to relax. Similarly once you begin to behave more confidently in the car, your feelings of anxiety should reduce and feelings of confidence return. Be warned though, there is usually a brief time lag (10 minutes or so) between behaving confidently ("walking the talk") and feeling confident.

c) Distraction

Certain situations, such as roundabouts and busy junctions draw our attention and build our anxiety because of the way fear drives our thinking.
If you notice a tendency to be over-vigilant at certain parts of a journey, your challenge is to must deliberately remove the excessive vigilance, or look away. For example, you might distract yourself form looking in the rear view mirror when stationary, by looking at people on the pavement, and asking yourself: "Where are they going? Why did they choose to wear that this morning?" Look at the houses, and see which need re-painting. In short, while it is safe to do so, focus your mind on anything that will direct your attention away from a supposed 'threatening' situation.

As we have said, relaxation is also a form of distraction – whilst you are concentrating on locating tension in you body and working on reducing it, you can't be over-attending to what's happening outside the car.

Reducing safety-seeking behaviour as a driver

As a driver, you have only one real strategy apart from keeping yourself as relaxed as possible, this being **partial response prevention** or cutting down unnecessary checking. For example, if you feel tempted to or over-check the mirrors, limit yourself to checking only at times when it is necessary e.g. when maneuvering. You could count the number of times you check on a given journey, and if it is excessive, try to reduce this number over time, to a more reasonable (but still safe) amount.

Use rational thinking to tackle your fears about reducing excessive safety-seeking behaviour (see Chapter 6).

Chapter 7. Reducing safety-seeking behaviour

> **Case Example:**
>
> Simon had felt nervous driving in built-up areas, ever since his car was shunted from behind while driving in town. In order to feel safer at the junction in town, he checked the mirror 23 times.
>
> He felt that he should keep an eye on the traffic pulling up behind so that he could take evasive action if another vehicle was about to shunt his.
>
> However, in practice, excessive mirror-checking made him feel anxious, as he saw every vehicle pulling up behind as a potential hazard. Furthermore, he was not focusing on the road ahead, which put him at risk of causing an accident himself.
>
> After challenging the necessity for this behaviour (see Chapter 6), Simon gradually reduced the frequency of "unnecessary mirror checks while stationary". He used the following challenge to give himself confidence:
>
> *"Checking the rear view mirror when stationary gives me no safety advantage, and may interfere with my ability to concentrate on the road ahead."*

If you are spending a lot of time planning and preparing for journeys, ask yourself "What am I frightened of?" If you fear getting lost, ask yourself "What is the worst that will happen?", and then ask yourself how likely is this to happen, and explore your options for managing your fears, while at the same time not avoiding the journey by car.

Chapter 7. Reducing safety-seeking behaviour

Case Example:

Jill was involved in a collision with an oncoming car on a sharp bend. She had her children in the car at the time. No-one was injured, but it was a terrifying experience. After the accident she gradually returned to driving, but found that she continues to swerve to the right when she saw oncoming traffic approaching, particularly if this was on a bend.

Fear provoking thought	Challenge
Oncoming traffic is going to hit me	Is there an alternative way of looking at this?
	Does this safety behaviour really reduce the risk?
	Is there a problem with this safety behaviour?

Response
Looked at another way, my swerving right on corners is potentially dangerous, and makes me feel anxious every time I drive round a bend, or see an oncoming car.

Before my accident I had driven round numerous bends (probably thousands) without swerving to the right, and had survived them safely without any impact. The probability of another impact on a corner is most likely to be less than I predicted.

Treatment Plan
Practice "standing my ground" on corners, ie. Driving normally and in the centre of my lane.

Key Points from Chapter 7:

- Safety-seeking behaviours are common after accidents.
- While making you feel safer in the short term, in the long term these behaviours maintain your fears.
- Being over-cautious can put you in danger.
- Challenges can be used to tackle the thinking behind safety-seeking behaviour, and to support a program of "weaning yourself off" excessive safety seeking.
- Reducing excessive safety-seeking behaviour should be tackled in a graded way or "one step at a time"

Chapter 8

Facing the fear

In order to overcome your fear of car travel, **you must enter the feared situation**, armed with the skills you have been practicing above. Facing your fear is the most powerful step you can take towards overcoming it.

Although the idea of facing your fear may sound alarming, you can build up your confidence gradually, using a graded step-wise approach. Graded practice allows you to discover that your fear gradually decreases and your confidence in the car will increase. Practicing being in a situation which makes you feel anxious and uncomfortable in the short-term, can make you feel more relaxed and confident in the long-term.

Figure 8.1. shows what happens to you anxiety when you face your feared situation e.g. being in a queue of traffic. If you escape or avoid the queue as soon as you feel fear, your anxiety decreases in the short-term, but you remain frightened of queues, and the fear comes back next time

Chapter 8. Facing the fear

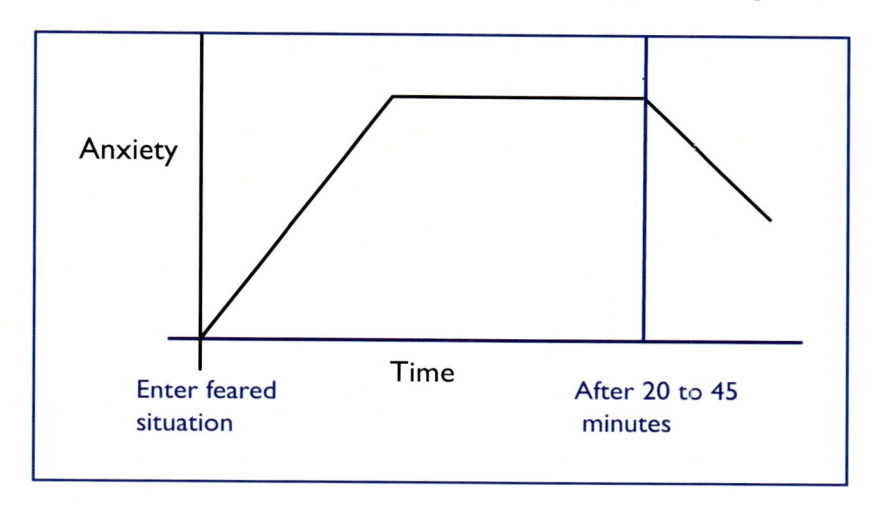

[Figure: Graph showing Anxiety vs Time. Anxiety rises from "Enter feared situation", plateaus, then declines "After 20 to 45 minutes".]

FIGURE 8.1

However if you practice being in the queue and 'ride the wave' of anxiety without escaping, your anxiety gradually fades without needing to escape. Your anxiety will not decrease as quickly as if you 'escape' but over time, as Figure 8.2 shows, if you practice regularly (ideally as soon as possible after the first practice), your anxiety will reduce further and further, and this reduction should be more or less permanent. By remaining in the feared situation, you are teaching yourself that it is safe e.g. to stay in a queue of traffic.

Facing your fear is a challenge, as you will have to tolerate the unpleasant physical feelings associated with fear (see Chapter 2). Remember, your system has become over-sensitive to these driving-related situations, seeing them as more dangerous than they really are. Your fear system is trying to protect you. Unfortunately it is exaggerating the risk (like the car alarm going off in the wind). To gear it down and re-educate your system, you will need to resist the urge to remove yourself from the situation.

With repeated practice, the peak of the 'wave' of anxiety will be lower, and the fear will come down more quickly.

Chapter 8. Facing the fear

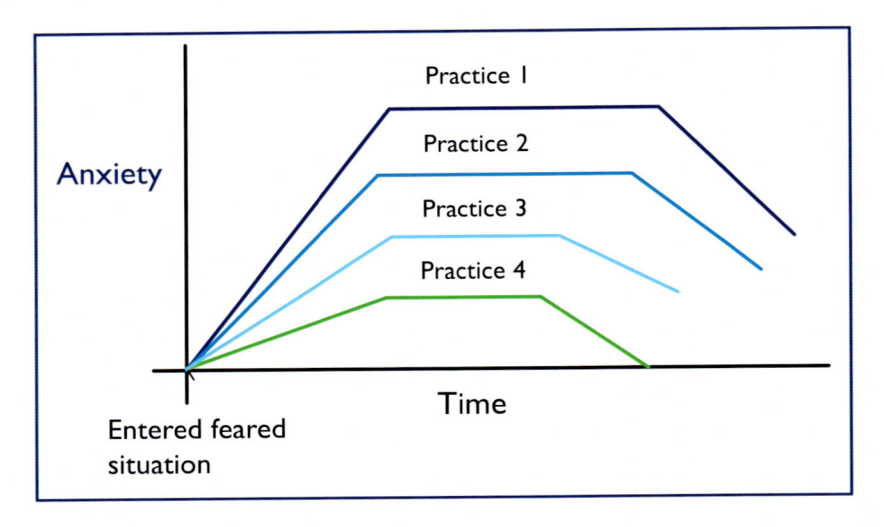

FIGURE 8.2

It is important that facing your fears is done in a graded and properly organized way. The following steps should be followed carefully.

Step 1: Set goals

Ask yourself what you would like to be able to do, if you were not frightened of car travel. Give yourself short-term and longer-term goals. Break down each goal into stages, or steps e.g.

GOAL 1: TO BE ABLE TO DRIVE TO SEE MY FRIEND IN TOWN ON MY OWN

- Practice driving in quiet lanes with my partner
- Build up to more built up areas
- Practice driving in quiet lanes alone
- Build up to driving alone in more built up areas
- Practice driving to town with my partner
- Drive to town on my own

By doing this, you have constructed what we call a 'hierarchy' – a list of situations from least to most difficult.

Step 2: Build a fear hierarchy

Begin by drawing up a list of driving situations and grade them in terms of how difficult they would be. Below we have set out a 10 step hierarchy – yours might have more or less steps in it. The steps might be the same as the goals you've just set out.

Be specific about each step, outlining the situation, time of day, whether you are alone or not, which seat in the car, etc. Write down the easiest challenge at step 1, and then work up in to more difficult situations as you go up the list. Rate the level of anxiety anticipated at each step in the right hand column using the following 0-10 scale:

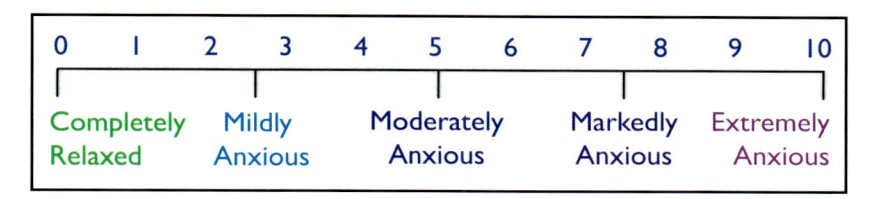

```
0    1    2    3    4    5    6    7    8    9    10

Completely   Mildly        Moderately      Markedly      Extremely
Relaxed      Anxious       Anxious         Anxious       Anxious
```

You may be starting from scratch, in that you are not driving at the moment, or you may be already driving, albeit in a limited way. If you are already driving, the steps should be arranged to take you beyond what you are already comfortable with in order to challenge yourself.

You will not be moving on to more challenging steps until you are comfortable with those situations lower down the hierarchy. To ensure that you experience success, make the gaps between each step small, not too difficult. After completing the first 10 steps, you may want to try another ten. It doesn't matter how many steps you have. The principle is to raise your anxiety a little bit at each step, and master it gradually, bit by bit.

Below is an example of Carol's fear hierarchy (see Chapter 3). Note the carefully graded challenges on her list.

Chapter 8. Facing the fear

Hardest	Predicted anxiety rating 0-10
10. Passenger travel at night, country lanes to Mum's past site of accident.	10
9. Passenger travel daytime, main roads.	10
8. Country lanes to Mum's alone, busy, daytime, past site.	9
7. Country lanes to Mum's with friend daytime, busy (school pick up time) past site of acciden	8/9
6. Driving main road to town alone dark (35 mins + return).	8/9
5. Driving main road to garden centre with friend, dark (30 mins + return)	8
4. Driving to Mum's alone, country roads, quiet (35 mins).	7/8
3. Driving to town with friend, country roads, daytime, quiet (35 mins + return)	7
2. Driving to town alone daytime, main roads, quiet traffic (35 mins + return).	4
1. Driving to town with friend daytime, main roads, quiet traffic (35 mins + return).	3
Easiest	

NB. Carol reported that as she worked her way up the hierarchy, the predicted anxiety of greater challenges came down, as confidence with easier challenges grew.

Mini-hierarchies

To achieve one of the steps in the hierarchy, you may need to construct a mini-hierarchy – the steps you need to take to achieve one bigger step.

Example

John constructed a hierarchy when he began to avoid driving altogether – driving on the motorway was the situation he feared most, driving to the local shops was the situation he feared least. So, he constructed the following mini-hierarchy:

1. Sit in the car with the engine running (45 minutes).
2. Drive a few yards up the road (and sit in stationary car 45 minutes).
   Get someone else to bring the car back.
3. Drive 50 yards up the road (and sit in stationary car 45 minutes).
   Get someone else to bring the car back
4. Drive 50 yards up road and into side turning.
   Turn the car and drive back.
5. Drive to the junction at the end of the road turn left and into the next turning.
   Turn the car and drive back.
6. Drive round the block once
7. Drive twice round the block
8. Drive to local shops when there are few cars around
9. Drive to local shops when it is busier
10. Drive to local shops and come back the long way.

Each task lasted approximately 45 minutes, even if it meant just sitting in the car whilst stationary.

Chapter 8. Facing the fear

10 Step Hierarchy

Hardest	Anxiety rating 0-10
10.	
9.	
8.	
7.	
6.	
5.	
4.	
3.	
2.	
1.	
Easiest	

FIGURE 8.4

Step 3. Working at your hierarchy

Since the accident you may have only gone in the car when absolutely necessary, or when you have been forced to do so. By doing this, you may have lost control over what is happening to you, and your fear is controlling what you do. Now, you have to learn to take active control over your fear. This means that when you go in the car, instead of being dragged out by necessity, you go in the car when you decide.

Set your mind to working on this every day. If you can decide to go out twice a day then all the better. Think about how you can incorporate driving practice into your day-to-day activities. Stick to the following rules each time you practice:

- Practice steps on the hierarchy one at a time, easiest first.

- Practice **every day** for at least 45 minutes (or until your fear subsides).

- The first time you enter each step, rate how anxious your feel on a 0-10 scale, where 0 = 'no anxiety at all', and 10 = 'total panic'. Each time you go out and practice a step, rate how anxious you feel. Use a 'Homework Diary' like the one below. By using this anxiety scale you will have measure of how your anxiety is dropping.

- Move on to the next step once your peak anxiety for your current step has reduced to manageable levels (say 3 or less out of 10 on the anxiety scale – see Step 2).

- Try not to hesitate before a practice session, it will only wind you up. There is some truth in the idea that "(S)he who hesitates is lost".

- If you have a set back, **don't worry**. Simply move a level or two down the hierarchy to a level you feel comfortable with, and begin moving on again.

- Enlist the help of others for support when trying more difficult steps.

- Always praise yourself for what you have achieved. Don't think "Oh, it was really only a little thing, only something I could do before". Overcoming fear is never easy.

- Expect the odd setback. If, while working on your hierarchy, you find that one day your fear is higher than you can tolerate, you may need to drop down a level, and consolidate your gains before moving on to the next challenge. Your confidence may dip. Just go with it and build it up using the same steps as before

---

TOP TIP:

Think of building confidence as similar to building up strength and stamina for a marathon. You start by training gently but regularly until your legs and lungs get used to the challenge. As you get fitter, you build up to longer and faster runs. If your training schedule is interrupted you have to take a step back, and build up stamina again. It is the same with driving confidence. The important thing is to keep going, one step at a time, but DO KEEP GOING.

Homework Diary

Record what you do. By writing it down you create a record of progress for you and others to see. Plan the step for the next day the day before, and write it down. By doing this you are committing yourself – it is harder to avoid. See Carol's diary below. There is a sample diary for you to photocopy in the Appendix.

Chapter 8. Facing the fear

Start date:

Day	Homework Task	Anxiety before	Anxiety during	Anxiety after	Time on task	Comments
Tues	Drive to town with friend (35mins there and back)	5	5	2	1 hr	Quite nervous to start with, focused on not checking mirrors. Way home easier
Wed	" " "				1 hr	Able to talk and not worry about road
Thur	" " "				1 hr	Forgot about fears

Chapter 8. Facing the fear

Pitfalls to look out for when facing your fears

- DON'T BITE OFF MORE THAN YOU CAN CHEW

  Stick with a graded approach, and don't try to proceed too fast. Make sure your anxiety has dropped to a low point on the scale before you move on. If you bite off more than you can really chew, you may find that you get very anxious, and lose faith in what you have achieved.

- STAY IN THE SITUATION LONG ENOUGH

  Anxiety takes a while to drop. You will need to stay in the particular situation you are working at on your hierarchy for 30-45 minutes. If you leave the situation too quickly, before your anxiety has had the chance to drop, you are only reinforcing the vicious cycle of avoidance, by repeating the mistake of thinking "Only by getting out of this can my anxiety go away." In the short term, leaving will be a relief, but in the long-term escaping just reinforces the perception that the situation really was dangerous, and your fears are strengthened.

- BE SURE OF YOUR RELAXATION SKILLS

  People who say relaxation "doesn't work" are those who have not practiced the skill properly or those who fail to attend to build-up of tension in their bodies because they are concentrating on safety-seeking behaviours. Try using relaxation skills daily, outside of your driving practice. Bringing down overall levels of tension will help with the challenges. Once you are really tense it takes more effort to relax yourself.

- WATCH OUT FOR `HIDDEN` SAFETY BEHAVIOURS

  Make sure that you are aware of all your safety behaviours. Check out with a friend what your behaviour is like in the car.

Safety-seeking behaviours serve as a subtle means of 'escaping' your feared situation. Make sure each challenge is 'clean' of excessive checking, holding on, or other avoidance (see Chapter 7).

- DELAYING PRACTICE

    Putting off practice, e.g. by making excuses, is a sign that you are still letting yourself be dominated by your anxiety. As we suggested above, commit yourself the day before what you are going to do, or plan out several days in advance. Write it down – it is less easy to avoid or put off.

- INFREQUENT PRACTICE

    Frequent practice is crucial. It is really important to repeat steps as soon as possible to reinforce your success. If you practice only once or twice a week, your progress will be much longer and drawn out.

- 'RIDING THE WAVE' OF ANXIETY

    Despite your relaxation, attempts at realistic thinking and distraction, you will find that you get anxious. Go with it, don't try to fight it – 'ride the wave' of anxiety. Just like any wave, it will lose its power as it goes along.

- NEGATIVE PREDICTIONS

    If you find yourself troubled by negative thoughts about what may happen when you go out in the car, then you haven't done your work on managing anxious thoughts properly. Go back through the exercises in Chapter 6 again. You may not have identified all your thoughts, or you may have tried to challenge them with things you simply can't believe at the moment. You may intellectually know it is safe e.g. to drive to town, but emotionally you feel afraid. Your feelings may take time to catch up with

Chapter 8. Facing the fear

what you know to be true. Similarly, for many people, it is only possible to feel confident in the car (or any situation for that matter), once you behave confidently.

- SET BACKS: IF AT FIRST YOU DON'T SUCCEED ...

You will almost certainly have little setbacks. It is in the nature of the beast that is anxiety for it to fluctuate for no real reason that you can see. It is also highly likely that things that happen occasionally will upset you – the car that comes just that bit too close, the heavy rainfall on the way home. If you suddenly find that you've gone back a bit – don't despair. You've done it once, you can do it again ... all is not lost. Don't be discouraged. Simply start again a bit further down the hierarchy at the point you were when you had your upsurge of anxiety. You may well find you regain confidence lost more quickly this time

Key Points from Chapter 8:

- Facing your fear is essential for you to feel more confident.
- Practice is most effective if it is carried out in a graded way, starting with less anxiety provoking situations and moving up.
- Practice should be repeated (every day) and prolonged (at least 45 minutes), or until your fears have subsided.
- It is important to watch out for hidden safety seeking behaviours which may contaminate your practice and delay your recovery.
- If you have a setback, just re-group, and re-start your program to build up your confidence again.

Chapter 9

Getting professional help

Not everybody with fear of car travel needs professional help in order to overcome their fears. However, regaining your confidence is quite a challenge. Whether or not you will need help will depend on the severity or nature of the accident you were in and on how severe your reactions to it have been. Painful injuries may have an impact, and you may require help with pain management (see Resources for further reading).

If your fear of car travel is so strong that you cannot get started on the strategies described above, then it is advisable to seek the support of a therapist. You may require some remedial driving lessons with an instructor who is experienced working with anxious drivers. Most driving schools will be able to recommend an instructor with specialized experience helping nervous drivers.

A proportion of accident survivors suffer from Post-Traumatic Stress Disorder (see Glossary). If symptoms of PTSD persist for more than a month after the accident, it is advisable to seek professional help.

Most emotional reactions to accidents and other traumas can be helped by therapy. There are many types of therapy available, but research shows that Cognitive Behavioural Therapy (CBT) is the most effective type of talking treatment for anxiety (see Glossary). Treatment tends to be short-term (between 6 and 12 sessions). CBT is a collaborative talking treatment. Your therapist may use many of the techniques described in this booklet.

Chapter 9. Getting professional help

If after reading this booklet, you feel you may need professional help, do not see this as a sign of weakness. Being wise enough to realize that you need more support to face the challenge of regaining your confidence, is a great strength.

A good starting point in trying to locate a therapist is your doctor. Cognitive Behavioural Therapy should be available on the NHS, usually via your local hospital's psychology or psychiatry department. Different kinds of mental health professionals are trained as CBT therapists – clinical psychologists, clinical nurse specialists, and psychiatric nurses. It is important when finding a therapist that you check that they have a further training in CBT, and experience working with accident survivors. If your doctor does not seem to understand your request, or does not know how to get you help, then you should ask for a second opinion from a different doctor.

Waiting lists for many NHS hospitals are lengthy. If a long wait for treatment is likely to make things difficult for you, you should alert your doctor to this as there may a way for you to be seen as a priority.

If you can afford to pay, you can locate a private therapist. As in the NHS, be sure you that your therapist is properly qualified and experienced in providing CBT for driving fears. A recent innovative approach to overcoming fears is the use of interactive self-help computer program. In particular a program called "Fearfighter" has been found to be useful in providing strategies for overcoming specific fears. Contact addresses for the relevant specialist organizations are given in the Resources section.

Final thoughts

Whether you are working on your fears independently or with the help of a therapist, remember to stick at it. Ultimately, neither this booklet, nor your therapist can do the work of overcoming your fears. Success depends on your efforts. Hopefully the techniques described here will help you to achieve this success with the least discomfort possible.

Remember if your fears become intolerable, you should see your doctor and try to get professional help. Even with help, setbacks in progress are normal, and should be seen as an opportunity to learn about your fears, and try again. With gradual, persistent effort you should be able to build up your confidence and get "Back in the Driving Seat". Good luck!

And really finally… If you have any comments or feedback from your reading or use of this booklet, we should be very pleased to hear them. Feel free to contact us directly at info@cbtnetworks.com, or visit our website http://www.cbtnetworks.com

Glossary

Cognitive Behavioural Therapy

Cognitive Behavioural Therapy is a talking treatment in which client and therapist work together to identify and understand particular difficulties. A practical, present-focused and collaborative style is used to develop and understanding of problems in terms of the relationship between thoughts, feelings and behaviour. A list of personalized, time-limited treatment goals is developed along with strategies for change. This approach can be used to help anyone irrespective of ability, culture, race or gender.

CBT is more than counselling. In traditional counselling, individuals are offered the opportunity to talk over their problems. Although this can be helpful in allowing people to "get things off their chest", it does not deal with the specific symptoms of driving phobia. Research shows that CBT is effective in helping people to tackle anxiety.

CBT is a brief treatment (6-10 sessions), and should be carried out by specialised health professionals. Treatment should be available on the NHS, by referral from your GP. However there may be long lists for therapy. Alternatively, if you can afford to pay, or have health insurance, you may want to consider a private therapist. Whichever route you choose it is important to ensure that your therapist is properly qualified, receives regular supervision, and has experience treating accident survivors. A list of relevant contact addresses is given at the back of this booklet.

Phobia

A phobia is an intense fear. The person avoids the situation or will only endure it with dread.
The treatment of phobias now has a long and often successful history with psychological methods.

Post-Traumatic Stress Disorder

Post-Traumatic Stress Disorder, or PTSD for short, is the name given to a combination of reactions to a trauma. The symptoms commonly seen after a trauma include: Nightmares, flashbacks to the memory of the trauma, anxious thoughts about the trauma, fear and avoidance of reminders or the trauma, irritability, poor sleep, and loss of interest in sex. Almost everyone has these symptoms after a trauma, but if they are severe or last for more than 1 month then they are given the name PTSD. If you have these symptoms you are not abnormal, but you have experienced an extreme and unexpected event and your system has not yet come to terms with it.

Resources

Order your own Relaxation Tape

How to Relax by Helen Kennerley
A short package, consisting of a relaxation tape, and an instruction sheet, which guides the user through a series of relaxation exercises.
Available for £2.50 from
The Booklets Secretary,
Psychology Department, Warneford Hospital,
Oxford OX3 7JX.
Tel.: 01865 223 986

Contact addresses

British Association for Behavioural and Cognitive Psychotherapies (BABCP)
The Globe Centre,
PO Box 9,
Accrington BB5 0XB.
Tel.: ++4 (0) 1254 875 277
Email: babcp@babcp.com   Website: www.babcp.com
The BABCP has a register of all approved CBT psychotherapists i.e. mental health professionals with specialized training in CBT.

British Psychological Society (BPS)
St Andrews House,
48, Princess Road East.
Leicester LE1 7DR
Tel: ++4 (0) 116 254 9568
The BPS has a register of all approved Chartered Clinical Psychologists. These will have undergone the necessary training to be able to help you.

CBT Networks
P.O. Box 566,
Banbury OX16 6AT.
Email: info@cbtnetworks.com   Website: www.cbtnetworks.com
A private independent treatment agency, with a bank of fully trained and accredited CBT therapists nationwide. CBT Networks will find a qualified CBT therapist close to home.

Fearfighter
www.fearfighter.com
A computerized self-help package for fears and phobias

Further reading

COPING SUCCESSFULLY WITH PAIN, by Neville Shone. Published 1992 by Sheldon Press. SPCK, Marylebone Road, London NW1 4DU

OVERCOMING TRAUMATIC STRESS – A SELF-HELP GUIDE USING COGNITIVE-BEHAVIOURAL TECHNIQUES, by Claudia Herbert and Ann Wetmore, published 1999 by Constable & Robinson Publishing Ltd., London

LIVING WITH FEAR: UNDERSTANDING AND COPING WITH ANXIETY (Second Edition) by Isaac Marks. Published 2001 by McGraw-Hill

PANIC DISORDER: THE FACTS (Second Edition), by Rachman & Da Silva. Oxford Press

HOMEWORK DIARY

Start date:

0	1	2	3	4	5	6	7	8	9	10
Completely Relaxed		Mildly Anxious			Moderately Anxious		Markedly Anxious		Extremely Anxious	

DAY	HOMEWORK TASK	anxiety before	anxiety during	anxiety after	Time on task	COMMENT

CBT NETWORKS Back in the Driving Seat